PESKY POEMS

By

T. L. Needham

Pesky
Poems

By
T. L. Needham

NF
MEDIA
LLC
~ no fear ~

Publisher

Printed in the United States of America

To contact the author or publisher:
Email: needham@accessus.net

ISBN: 978-0-578-00180-7

Contents:

1   Poetry

2   Pesky Poem

4   Heavenly Cupcakes

6   Lucky the Cat

8   Duck Dance

9   Cat Woman

10   Reigning Cats and Dogs

12   Spider Moon

14   Frog Song

15   Story Time

16   Doctor T. Bear

17   Mother Loves Me

18 She's My Girl

19 Rock Skipper

20 Seeing You

21 Blue Mail

22 Someone I Can Trust

23 Always

24 The Moon and the Stars

25 Home Coming

26 Unconditionally Yours

27 A Key Lost and Found

28 And So You Love Me

30 Maybe

31   Forevermore

32   Girl Clothes and Red High Heels

33   The Cottonwood Tree

34   On the Level

35   A Horny Life

36   True Believer

36   Clearly Perfect

37   Born Again

38   Memories

39   Cup Cake

40   Mind over Matters

41   Free Secrets

42   First & Last Impressions

43   The Eternal Moment

44   White Sheets

46   Biscuit Eater

46   Come On

47   My Brothers Voice

48   Old Sol

49   Significant

50   Feeling Alive

51   Wake Up Call

52   Blue Bird Hill

57   Kitty Claus

64   Cupid's Arrow

65   Faithful Sunflower

66   First Born

67   In Between

68   Free Advice

72   Unreasonable

73   PLEASE

PESKY POEMS

By

T. L. Needham

Poetry

I cannot think
Of anything
More important
Than poetry.

For what else
Has man conceived
That renders the soul
Transparent?

And, without a soul —
What else would . . .
Matter?

Pesky Poem

There is a poem inside me . . .
It wants to get out.
But I just ignore it.
It sighs with a pout.

It was born in my heart,
Deep in my chest.
But I just ignore it,
Like all the rest.

But this one's determined.
It won't go away!
It haunts me and taunts me . . .
Says, "I'm here to stay . . ."

Still, I am too busy —
Just can't find the time,
To pay much attention
To this silly old rhyme.

So I buried it somewhere
In the back of my mind,

That vast wasteland where
Things get lost all the time.

But this pesky poem,
It won't go away,
It keeps coming back —
Says, "I'm here to stay."

So the sly little poem
Said, "I'll find a way out!"
As it looked thru my eyes —
And peeked out of my mouth.

Then — without warning,
It gave me the slip!
I picked up a pen
And it leaked out the tip!

Now it's outside me —
My poem went away.
Now it's in your mind . . .
Says, "I'm here to stay."

Heavenly Cupcakes

Along came a bakery truck
Bounding down the road,
It hit a bump and lost
Half its load!

A pretty frosted cupcake
Flew up in the air,
And landed at the feet
Of a Jackrabbit hare.

The cupcake took a bounce
Across the road it fell —
And landed on a Turtle's back,
Right on top its shell!

The Turtle disappear! Right —
Tight into his shell,
And there set the cupcake,
Just where it fell.

Across the road, the Rabbit hopped,
And to the Turtle yelled . . .
"Cupcakes are falling from Heaven!
And, you're hiding in your shell!"

The Turtle took a moment,
And peeked out just a bit . . .
Saw the Rabbit eating cupcake
And joined right in . . . you bet!

Lucky the Cat

Lucky the Cat!
That's my name,
Patrolling the jungle,
That's my game.

Pity the mouse
That crosses my path —
Blue Jays and squirrels,
Meet their aftermath.

Napping and purring
Are favorite past times.
My next can of cat food
Is always in mind.

With two friendly dogs
My home I share . . .
And leftover cat food,
That's all I can spare!

But Lucky I am!
Shall I tell you why?
I have a pet human
Who lights up my sky.

She speaks cat talk
With never a flaw.
Her "meow" is special —
I come when she calls.

I roll over with joy
And purr all the time,
Then rub 'round her ankles
To show she is mine.

Duck Dance

Christina and Albert were friends of mine,
Two of the best I've ever had.
Often as I could I'd visit them.
To see me they always seemed glad.

But sometimes I'd have to call them,
And they always appeared when I quacked!
Soft flakes of white bread I'd feed them,
And watch them paddle this way and that.

Often they did a cute duck dance,
Swimming and bobbing in tight unison,
As if to say, "We are mates for life,
And seeing you is always such fun!"

Yet winds chilled, and days grew short,
Under a grey winter sky . . .
They just left one day, without a word,
Not even saying goodbye . . .

Yet, I believe they shall return
When the spring song birds sing,
So my eyes I keep upon the sky . . .
And listen — *for the flutter of wings.*

Cat Woman

Women are a lot like cats!

Now you see it!
Now you don't!

Yes, I will —
No, I won't!

Let me in . . .
No — Let me out!

Pay close attention,
Or, I sit and pout . . .

Can I help you?
If you please?

Well, I won't!
But, I'll taunt and tease.

Don't you just love me?
Here's a little squeeze.

Reigning Cats and Dogs

Cats are king!
Nothing is more true.
They are better than dogs,
But that's nothing new.

So says all cats
Who take it as so.
We are quiet, and soft,
And a pleasure to hold,
And we hardly ever
Give cause to scold.
So, that makes cats best
When it's all told.

But no! Says all dogs —
Let us have our say!
Who is more fun
To take out and play?
Who licks you face
And jumps in your way
Whenever you appear?
To say, "I missed you all day!"

Well, this is too hard
To decide which is a jest!
So a cat and a dog
In each home is best.

Spider Moon

Sitting on my patio
Late one summer night,
Staring at the full moon
And basking in its light,
A glimpse of something small
Saw I, across the moon's face dart . . .
And then again the other way —
It gave me quite a start!
Again and again, I watch it glide
Across that glowing orb,
Into its task a little spider
Was totally absorbed.
Stringing cables of silver silk
Across and back again, so soon —
It became quiet clear to me,
He had designs upon the moon!
He could not stand to see it free,
So back and forth he came,
Spinning circles in his web,
So perfect in design and frame.

Beneath the shadow of a Redbud's leaf
In silent wonder did I sit
And stare in utter disbelief —
As he caught the moon within his web . . .
And held it tight with all his feet!
Eight legs stretched as far as might,
Grabbed the moon from side to side —
And held it motionless that night . . .
Just for an instant, that was all!
And then he set it free . . .
Then, knowing he could do it —
He set his eyes on me!
And I, now knowing well his abilities,
Took no chances, no not me —
Removed myself from the spider's view
And, into my house did flee!

Frog Song

No so long ago —
At the bottom of the hill,
A little creek passed by
Where frogs did eat their fill,
And sit and croak all night,
Or leap into the stream,
Just to make a splash,
Or create a big scene!

A noisy place to visit!
But it was always fun
To catch a glimpse of them
Just basking in the Sun.
But now they are all gone —
And have been for awhile,
So one begins to wonder
Why the frogs made us smile?

Was it something they all knew . . .
That made them leave this place?
And will we be the last to learn
The fate of the human race?

Story Time

Tell me a story Daddy dear,
Before I go to bed,
Of spooks and goblins, scary things —
To fill my heart with dread.

Or better still, of castles and kings,
A knight on a great white horse —
Yes, happy things to fill my dreams,
That would be better, of course!

Don't make me go upstairs alone.
There's something under my bed —
And without a story to protect me,
My feet just turn to lead!

So tell me a story Daddy dear?
Or, I will never go to bed!
It's not that I'm not sleepy,
But, the darkness that I dread . . .

Doctor T. Bear

I felt an ache in all my joints,
And fever flushed my face,
I could not breathe out of my nose,
And my heart just seemed to race.

I'm sick," I told my little girl,
Who took pity upon me,
And offered her sure remedy —

" Just go to bed, Daddy dear,
And curl up with my Teddy Bear."

Mother Loves Me

Mother loves me, I can tell,
And shall I tell you why?
Home from school I stayed today,
She knows I would not lie.
My stomach aches, my tongue is green,
I think I'm going to die . . .
On top of that — my homework's due!
But that's not the reason why,
Going to school just makes me sick!
And that's the truth — no lie!
So I'm home today — what's on TV?
Say Mom, may I have a piece of pie?

She's My Girl

Butterflies land on her shoulder,
And I've heard the angels sing
As she'd walk down the sidewalk,
Or touch heaven from her swing.

I've seen her heal a puppy —
By just holding it in her hand,
And bring life back to a chipmunk,
As if God and she shared a plan.

She's my girl —
She means everything to me.
She was the answer to a prayer,
When God said, "Let her be . . ."

She can jump a horse over a fence
Or, they can stand just perfectly still.
I've seen her waltzing on a mare,
To watch her ride is always a thrill.

I've taught her everything I know,
From skipping rocks to driving a car.
We even read some poetry,
There is no doubt — she'll go far . . .

She is my girl —
She means everything to me.
She always makes me proud —
She is the best I'll ever see.

Rock Skipper

Would you believe me
If I said rocks can fly?
And walk on water?
It is no lie.
It is all in the wrist,
With help from the eye.
Set just the right angle
And let the rock fly!
Across the water
It will skip and slide
And with help from you
Make it to the other side.
So have faith my friend --
And just give it a try.
Pick your rocks carefully,
You'll find one that can fly!

Seeing You

Short notice — bad timing,
Or what can it be
That keeps me from you . . .
Who I most want to see?

Perhaps it's a dream,
And I never knew,
To get us together,
Would be so hard to do.

Then maybe it's just
The way it must be,
And you'll always remain
Someone I wanted to see.

Blue Mail

A letter from you,
That will brighten the day,
Just hearing your voice
In my mind have your say.

Perhaps a surprise!
A package or two.
Or, just a postcard
That says, "I miss you . . ."

And maybe that check
That is long over due!
But, please — no more bills,
I can barely make do!

Yet, the mailbox is empty
And that's nothing new,
Expecting all this . . .
I found only the blues.

Someone I Can Trust

I will think of you
Each morning when
The Sun warms my face.

I will remember you
Each time I hear the
Laughter of a child . . .

I will think of you
Each time I seek
Love's light in happy eyes.

I will remember you
Whenever I meet
One who seeks understanding.

I will think of you
When I am angry
At one who craves forgiveness.

I will remember you
When I am alone
And hunger for a friend.

I will think of you
When I close my eyes
Needing someone I can trust.

Always

You were always there
    In my mind.

I knew you were mine
    All the time.

Waiting for me somewhere
    Down the line.

Around every corner,
    Behind every door,

I searched all my life --
    Not sure what for. . .

Until I saw you --
    The one I adore.

The Moon and the Stars

Once upon a time,
Not so long ago,
I made a wish upon the moon
And all the stars a glow.

A secret wish . . .
That forever you'd be mine
And that our love
Would endure to the end of time.

Well, they heard my wish,
And in their glow, it did come true.
So now in thanks to the moon and stars,
And to you my love, I give them all to you.

Home Coming

I'm coming home Honey!
And I've missed you all day.
So you better get ready,
Cause it's time to play.

Yes, I 'm coming home,
I could sure use a drink,
Plus some good loving,
So what do you think?

Cause I'm coming home
Like your angel from above
Who needs you right now . . .
So, get ready for love!

Unconditionally Yours

There is only one
Way to love —
Totally, completely,
Unconditionally.

There is only
One way to forgive —
Totally, completely,
Unconditionally.

If one does love,
Then one must forgive —
Totally, completely,
Unconditionally.

Only then is love eternal,
And forgiveness everlasting . . .
Totally, completely,
Unconditionally.

A Key Lost and Found

I found a key along my way
Shaped like a heart and pure
It was familiar to me,
I'd held it before, I'm sure.

With no delay — but certainty
I set out upon my quest,
To find the owner of the key,
Then touch it to her breast.

Her heart just opened up to me,
And the truest love out poured.
My love matched hers' in purity,
That a heart-shaped key restored.

And So You Love Me

How do I explain how much I love you?

Well, first — you are common as dirt.
And so am I, and so I love you.

And you make no pretense to be more,
And neither do I, and so I love you.

And you have known betrayal,
As so have I, and so I love you.

Yet not bitter, but willing to love again,
And so am I, and so I love you.

You honor your parents, and who they are,
And I do too — and so I love you.

You accept me as I am, and who I am,
And so I do you, and so I love you.

You play no games, but keep it real,
And so do I, and so I love you.

You are good and beautiful,
Yet know it not, and so I love you.

You love me without restraint,
As I do you too, and so I love you.

You value devotion and give it willingly,
And I do too, and so I love you.

You know love is unconditional,
And so do I, and so I love you.

You know love needs trust and respect,
And I know this too, and so I love you.

Your laugh, smile and voice gives me joy —
And I give it back too, and so I love you.

And I have loved you since I first saw you,
And you know this is true . . .
and so you love me!

Maybe

Maybe you will remember me
As I remember you, and loved
You, so very long ago.

And, maybe, if you remember me,
You will still remember how you felt,
In our early, tender, and innocent days.

Maybe you recall the woods we walked,
Our special cave, and moments together
Hand in hand, eye to eye, lips to lips.

And, maybe, remembering this
And even more, you will long
To see me again, as I long for you.

Then maybe, eye to eye,
And lips to lips, embraced in arms
Around each other again, maybe . . .

Just maybe, our love will bloom again,
Maybe, this time without bounds, our
Love will rise fully and forever!
Maybe.

Forevermore

Snow falling softly,
The lovely sound
Of complete silence
Fills my ears.

The hurt lingered so long,
Until you kissed me,
And made me laugh,
As love healed my soul.

Rain falling all day
Washing the dust of life
Off my mind, heart, and
Spirit—now all renewed.

You opened your door,
And said, "Come in . . ."
And let me love you —
Forevermore.

Girl Clothes and Red High Heels

I've love a woman
And she is so fine,
She knows how to
Please her man any old time.

She's a little bit country,
And that's just fine,
She wears blue jeans and
Cowboy boots most of the time.

But, when she's in the mood
To show how she really feels —
She puts on girl clothes
And red high heels!

Now take it from me
It's the real deal,
To love a woman wearing —
Girl clothes and red high heels!

Yes, that's a fact that
She makes the love so real,
When she puts on her
Girl clothes and red high heels!

So take it from me,
It will be lucky you feel,
If your loving woman's wearing —
Girl clothes and red high heels!

The Cottonwood Tree

I had a dream
And you did agree
That we should make love
Under a cottonwood tree.

So we picked a spot
Where no one could see
And before very long
We set our souls free!

And now but a memory
We will cherish with glee
That beautiful time
Under the cottonwood tree.

On the Level

The important tool,
If one would care,
Is a drop of water
With a bubble of air.

For it reveals all
And is always fair.
If it is done right —
It is always square,

And on the level,
But just beware —
If it is not so . . .
It will need repair!

A Horny Life

Here we are,
On the horns of a dilemma,
Leading our contradictory lives,
At the cutting edge of technology,
Leaving the good old days behind,
Day by day . . .
Before tomorrow comes —
It is too early,
Before it is too late.
Seize the moment!
For tomorrow . . . may never come!
For you, or I,
Or worse,
Alive still — to sort things out . . .
It will never happen!

True Believer

You lied to me.
And that is the truth.
Because you said it is so.
And I believed you.
And that is the truth.
Just to make it so.

Clearly Perfect

Let me make one thing
Perfectly clear
Just once.

Wait — I am coming,
Not now, Later.

I will get back
With you . . . Later.

Maybe . . . Never.

Born Again

My very soul . . .
In time suspended,
Did not know
Love's kiss commended.

For life's sweet gift,
Tho not my request,
Was thrust upon me
By love's bequest!

Since birth I have lived,
But it was not true,
This life began —
When I first saw you.

Memories

Of all things
In this life possessed,
It is the memories
That are the best.

They never wear out,
Or go out of style,
And they never fail —
To make the heart smile!

Yes, the richest source
Of personal wealth
Are those dusty memories
Sitting on the self . . .

And, the greatest hope
For each new day
Is one special moment —
That will never go away.

Cup Cake

Life is short,
Like a cup cake.

Life is sweet,
Like a cupcake.

But it is best
With lots of frosting,
Like a cup cake.

And when it is over,
There is only papers
And a few crumbs —
Like a cup cake.

Mind over Matters

Like water in a crystal bowl,
I can see clearly,
Light comes shining through,
The vessel looks empty, yet it is full.

The message is clear.
If you do not mind,
Nothing really matters.

And, if you do mind —
Everything matters.

Free Secrets

Are you a keeper of secrets?
Things no one else must know?
That makes you hide, or even lie,
To be sure the truth won't show?

Then you are trapped inside a web
That you yourself have spun,
And you live in fear they'll be known
By all who live under the Sun.

And secrets are expensive --
They cost the trust of all you know,
And those who love you will wish
You'd just let the truth be known.

Then just spill all your secrets
Upon the ground — a place for all to see!
So everyone can know the truth . . .
Only then are you set free.

First & Last Impressions

Bluebirds build their nests —
Are we being born again?

Our bed is made, fresh,
And new, but where are you?
Are we both alone . . . together?

I am not afraid to die.
I am afraid of being alive,
But not really living.

The Eternal Moment

The past exists
Only in a memory . . .

The future exists
Only in a dream . . .

Only the moment is real.
Do not let it pass — unfulfilled.

For memories can fade,
And dreams may perish . . .

But now, this instant, is reality!
This constant moment — *is eternal.*

White Sheets

Where is my mother?
Without her I am lost.
I need her right now,
But now she is lost.

Where is my mother?
I have looked everywhere,
In the house — her bedroom,
The kitchen — she is not there!

Where is my mother?
Does she know she is lost?
I've tried hard to find her,
In the chill of an early frost . . .

Where is my mother?
She is not in the house.
I will find her outside . . .
Am I the one who is lost?

Where is my mother?
I am too young to be alone.
Only yesterday — first steps I took,
Now she is gone . . . I walk alone.

Where is my mother?
Outside in the sunshine,

Have I found her at last,
Pinning white sheets on the clothes line?

Where is my mother?
I know she is there —
Moving among great white sails —
Billowing sheets and sun-lit cool air.

Where is my mother?
I caught a glimpse of her feet,
I am close to her now,
Beneath the last hanging white sheet.

Where is my mother?
Reaching up to the sky,
I saw her hands just now . . .
Pinning a white sheet — that just seemed to fly.

Where is my mother?
She was just there . . .
Then I stepped in to greet her,
There was nothing — but sunlight and air.

Where is my mother?
Set sail on sunlight and air,
Among billowing white sheets,
That's where she is . . . I know she is there.

Biscuit Eater

Nothing tastes better than a hot biscuit . . .
Warm and moist, firm outside, soft inside,
And, the best biscuit is made with love,
So it rises, and swells and asks to be buttered,
Then licked, and nibbled, and licked some more —
Until the biscuit opens wide into a heavenly
Invitation to have your fill, then say,
May I have another, Oh Please?

Come On

I am coming
Sooner than you think
And I shall be gone
Before you know it —
Don't wait up for me . . .

My Brothers Voice

I hear a voice
My brother said
It comes from within
Inside my head
I tried to ignore it
Lest I be mislead
I asked it to go
It persists instead
Only gets stronger
Fills my heart with dread
Who are you I asked
I am God it said
What are you doing
Inside my head
Is it your playpen
Where idle thoughts embed
You've nothing else to do
Not really — He said
Still I have things to do
And you I shall shed
It is my head you know
But my dreams have fled
Yet after all these years
The voice — still haunts my head

Old Sol

Beginning and ending
Each day with a glow,
Bringing warmth and light
To all creatures below.

Never failing to rise
As duty calls,
Without hesitation,
Whatever the cause

And always returning
To brighten our road,
Thru darkness and clouds —
In faith, you lighten our load.

Oh, what is the secret
Of your persistence?
Do you just never
Yield to resistance?

So, again there you go,
On your slow daily stroll,
Across the great blue sky . . .
Good morning — Old Sol!

Significant

You are a human being . . .
No more — and no less
Than countless millions
Who ever have — or now exist.

Yet, you are significant . . .
No more — or less,
Yet, still significant . . .
Nonetheless.

Significant — not,
By condition of birth,
Nor by the condition
Of your personal worth.

Significant — in prospects,
Potentials, and deeds,
Hopeful realizations
Of far-flung dreams.

Uniquely significant . . .
In the infinite mist,
Significant — simply
That you do exist.

Feeling Alive

I touch your heart
And invade your mind,
Sinking deep roots
Into your soul to find
The meaning of life —
The essence of being.
I keep on searching
Until at last seeing
A warm glow within —
Love's constant healing,
And then I shall know
Life begins by feeling . . .

Wake Up Call

She left this world at 3:15 A.M.
A very long time ago.
For years since, at that same time,
I awake abruptly from my slumber.
Then, alone in the darkness,
I remember her —
And we talk of many things . . .

The clock dial glowed 3:15 A.M.
This morning, I awoke again,
To the sound of a low emphatic thud,
As a morning newspaper hit my driveway!
Thrown by that same nocturnal messenger
Who calls me at this time each morning . . .
Bringing me news of another world.

Blue Bird Hill

The first time I saw the place
It took forever to get there.
Then I found myself
In the middle of no where. . .

At the end of a gravel road
With no place else to go,
On top of a hill and
Oh did the wind blow. . .

That never let up!
And for this you were glad,
For the place was the home
Of so many cats, it smelled bad!

House needs work too.
Or a dozer to knock it flat.
Just make a big hole
Where the house once sat!

There is an old barn.
Cats live there too,
But, I saw no mice,
Rats, nor other cat food.

A shallow old pond
With weeds gone to seed
Gave local mosquitoes
A fine place to breed.

Then a coal train comes by,
On tracks border the farm,
About every 30 minutes . . .
You will need no alarm!

So as I stood there,
Thinking the place's a disgrace . . .
A Bluebird flew by —
I said, "I will take this place!"

So we set about to make
This old house swell,
Gutted the entire interior,
Just to get rid of the smell.

It's a Baltimore Oriole . . .
I've wanted to see all my life.
Well, he showed up today
And even brought his wife!

She was there splashing
In the bird bath with wet joy,
Then flew into the Redbud,
And just sat there so coy.

Along came Mr. Oriole
Who took his turn to splash,
Then made love to his Mrs.
And was gone in a flash!

The birds just kept coming,
A bird lover's dream,
Goldfinches, Chickadees,
Even an Indigo Bunting was seen!

But that is not all!
No, not in the least . . .
Scarlet Tanagers, Vireos, and more,
It just never ceased.

Plus little furry creatures
Kept coming around,
Like possum, fox, gophers
And many deer all abound.

To the south was a view . . .
Made you just want to stare,
A sea of tall grass, big pond,
Far horizon — a sky so fair.

The home of four horses,
Ate grass to their fill,
And come a runnin' & buckin'
To the top of our hill.

Leonardo, an Arabian was black,
Between his eyes a white star.
All pride and potential,
You know he'll go far.

Hillary, an old Quarter horse mare
Was always in charge.
But don't tell young Leo
Cause he leads the charge!

Scout, a proud Paint —
Who just looked very fast,
All white, brown and black,
He'd never finished last.

There was a fourth horse,
Paint, all white & brown
Stayed close to Hillary
When we came around.

Sometimes we'd feed them
A fist of grass in our hand,
Or an apple or carrot.
This must be God's plan.

So these four horses,
Our neighbors for sure,
Became our first friends
On Blue Bird Hill, so pure.

Kitty Claus

It was on Christmas Eve, as I recall,
Not so long ago, a cat by the name of
Kitty Claws, the meanest cat I ever saw,
Learned what Christmas is all about.

His name he earned, there is no doubt,
From little mice, his favorite prey, who
Felt his claws and teeth in every bout,
To their everlasting dismay.

And on this Christmas Eve,
The family all in bed,
Hard as it is to believe
Left a fire glowing quite by chance!

Sat to complete the scene,
Upon the mantle Santa's treats —
And starving mice could only dream —
Was warm cookies and milk, as usual.

And Claws, not missing any beats,
Curled up to sleep upon the hearth
To feel the warmth and guard the treats,
Lest any mouse would attempt to eat . . .

Now all was quiet, and in the glow
Of warm red embers and Christmas lights,
There came a silent falling snow
Softly covering house, town and all.

And in this stillness, all were sleeping,
Except the thin little clan of mice,
Who knew the time for creeping —
Was now, if this night they'd be eating.

Yes, Santa's treats were meant for them,
Of this they were certain,
He'd understand when he saw how thin
They were in mean old Claw's jurisdiction.

So up the Christmas tree they scurried . . .
Father Matt, and little Luke, his son,
Who looked a little chubby, but is only furry —
Over skin and bones.

Then across both jumped onto the mantle
In one mighty leap, and barely kept from
Falling off — by grabbing hold on to a candle,
That nearly fell to where Claws did sleep!

"That was close!" Matilda prayed
To herself, as the mother mouse watched
With hope that Claws just stayed
Put and would not wake up . . .

Just then a crack and a pop was heard!
From the embers as they glowed —
And all mice watched without a word . . .
As an ember landed on Claws furry tail!

Only a moment passed, just long enough
To set Claw's tail on fire . . .
And then learn that Claws is not so tough!
As he let out a startled—Meeeoooww!

Around the room he raced in terror!
Nearly setting the tree on fire!
Not knowing that his only error . . .
Was not leaving his tail behind!

"He is doomed, I am sure!" Matilda cried,
To Matt upon the mantle.
"Just let him burn until he died,"
Cried Luke, who'd already lost his tail.

For Claws had nearly caught him . . .
Once, and surely would have then —
If Luke were not all fur and so very thin,
But Claws got his tail and nothing more!

Yet, Matt knew in his heart,
It was wrong to just stand by —
To watch one suffer wasn't smart,
And it just wasn't right!

So, just as Claws made a pass —
Flaming tail in hot pursuit!
Off the mantle Matt pushed the glass
Of milk down on poor Claw's back!

It did the trick and doused the flame
And also took all the cookies and the plate
And knowing they had lost the game —
Matt and Luke made a fast retreat.

There in the darkness of their den
Matt, Matilda, Luke and the babies all
Dreamed in hunger of what might have been
Had their Christmas only went differently.

As the snow continued to fall in silence,
A wondrous change came over Claws,
That made him feel more compliance,
As his mouse relations were concerned.

He recovered quickly from his fright —
No harm was done, but scorched tail fur,
And set to work that very night
To change his ways with lessons learned.

Christmas morning, at dawn's first glow,
The mice family awoke still so very hungry,
A feeling they had come to know —
But a scent of cookies filled the den . . .

Yes, and cheese, crackers and cream,
Set on a platter just outside their den,
Luke noticed first and let out a scream!
All awoke in disbelief of what's now seen.

Luke said, "Oh what a thrill!
Just look what Santa's left us!
Now we can eat our fill . . ."
But Matilda stopped him fast —

"Stop! she cried! "It could be a trap!"
You know how he is, cannot be trusted --
He is just a terrible cat!"
As she held Luke back by his tail.

"No dear, I think Claws has changed,
He is just sitting there smiling --
And looking really quite strange!"
Luke cried as she pulled on his tail.

"I think Dad is right, Matt also said,
"Claws would not just sit there --
Out in the open, if he wanted us dead,
And, I am so hungry, I want to be fed."

So, out went Luke, then Matt for a bite,
And Claws never moved, just purred,
Then he smiled with all his might!
As the mice ate their fill . . .

So next from the den,
Came Matilda and the babies
Each wearing only a grin,
As they all ate their fill.

Then Luke changed Claw's name
Right there on the spot,
"Santa and Claws are both the same,
So Kitty Claus is now his new name!"

And after all that,
They all became best friends —
Those mice and that cat,
So this is where our story ends . . .

Cupid's Arrow

Pops been gone a long time,
But you still know he is near,
Cause you can hear his voice
Like he just whispered in your ear.

Mom's been gone even longer,
Yet, her voice seems so clear —
You hear her laugh and happy voice
As she whispers, "Have no fear . . ."

For they both say, "Love surrounds you,"
And it will throughout the year —
Since they are playing Cupid . . .
And their love arrow hit me my dear!

Faithful Sunflower

At night the Sunflower never sleeps,
But spends the night turning to the
East to greet the rising Sun, in it's
Full glory — then to follow the Sun
Across the sky all day, east to west,
Face to face, Sun to Sunflower,
Until sunset at each days' end.

Yes, the Sunflower will never rest,
Always turning, waiting, in hope,
For the next new day — to face
Again the rising Sun . . .
To match its beauty to the Sun's
And show that all is constant,
And beautiful, on Earth . . . as long as
A faithful Sunflower faces each new day.

First Born

I was a child myself,
When you left the baby shelf —
So totally without a clue,
I mean me, not you —

Old enough to war, but not to drink,
Yet your Dad, which truly made me think.
But, you were loved all the same,
The first born to our family name.

How much you loved to draw —
Especially with lipstick on the wall!
But art was natural for you,
Just as your beauty was natural too.

Yet, you bore the brunt of my mistakes,
And many others who were flakes.
It made you strong, to forget, forgive all
Those hurtful things that made you fall . . .

And you are truly loved for all these things,
By me, and all, including angels upon wings.
So never doubt what you can do
And never let the past make you blue.

In Between

You hardly made a scene
Not the first, not the last,
You did come in between.

Quiet and listened to all I said,
And so slow to finish dinner,
But quick to go to bed.

There you hid your precious toys
Under the mattress, far as could reach,
To keep safe, what gave you such joys.

Love and hurts both came to you,
So you had to grow up fast, and
It made you stronger, yet so pretty too!

Keen awareness of all about you,
And your beauty from within, so soon
You knew life and all the good you'd do.

Now, when life offers you a choice . . .
Positive or negative, but not in between,
You'll smile or laugh, in your happy voice!

Free Advice

Ignore that spider you see
Out the corner of your eye.
It is not really there, maybe,
But do call the exterminator.

There is really nothing and
No one under your bed.
Trust me, I have looked
Every night for over sixty years.

But, do not forget to check
Your closets too, just in case —
They may not fit under your bed
Aliens, monsters, all . . . too big!

Credit cards are God's
Intelligence test for all of us.
He gave us free will,
But WILL POWER is up to us.

Do not ever spend all
Your money, save some
For that rainy day —
Then go out and spend it all!

Speed limits are for our
Own protection, from ourselves,
Each other, bored Cops
And another rule to break!

Worry not, it is a waste of time,
You can do almost nothing
About hardly anything,
Just make decisions and be happy.

Maintain your car, and your body —
One gets you where you're going
The other keeps you going
Until you get there, and then some too.

Dogs give so much more than they take,
They love and protect us.
Cats give little and take little too,
But they are quiet, and so soft!

Listen close, talk less,
Ask lots of questions,
Make no harsh judgments of others,
And ignore it when they do of you.

Go to school, not to gain knowledge,
But to learn the joy of learning.
Then you will never stop learning,
Which you must do to live well.

Listen to those who disagree with you —
They might actually be right!
But, you will never know until you listen,
And debating is such fun too!

Why is it so hard to heed
Our parent's good advice?
Is it that making our own mistakes
Is more fun and so instructive too?

Every single child matters most,
They carry the seeds of tomorrow.
So get on your knees, join their world,
Engage them eye to eye, you will see the future!

Honor your parents, and ancestors,
You are nothing without them.
You will know the sacrifice they made for you,
When you have kids too.

Read at least one poem
Every single day, to lift your spirits,
Inspire your heart to love, your mind to
Think — you may find a poet within you.

As often as you can, walk a beach,
Take a ride out into the country,
Take a long walk in the woods,
Find a big lake and take a boat ride.

Get your hands dirty in a garden,
Dirt is what we are, Dust to Dust . . .
Make something grow and watch it
Bring new life into your own life.

Do that thing today, that you always
Wanted to do, put it off no longer,
No matter what it takes to have
Anything that makes you happy.

Dare to dream what you can be, but set
Goals, make a plan, and then take action —
Only then, by working your plan each day
 . . . *will all your dreams come true.*

Unreasonable

I did not write this poem . . .
        to make money.

I did not write this poem . . .
        to be funny.

I did not write this poem . . .
        to be cool.

I did not write this poem . . .
        to be cruel.

I did not write his poem . . .
        to just profess.

I did not write this poem . . .
        to just confess.

I did not write this poem . . .
        to make you glad

I did not write this poem . . .
        to make you sad.

I did not write this poem . . .
        to teach a lesson.

I did not write this poem . . .
        to keep you guessing.

I did not write this poem . . .
        to have a ball.

I wrote this poem —
        For no reason at all!

PLEASE

Please protect planet earth.
Love all it is and ever will be.
Earth is our home, always and forever.
And, it is all we have, or ever will.
Save it for us, our children and theirs.
Environment gives life, but we must give it back.